ANIMALS LOST & FOUND

Illustrated by
Jonathan Woodward

Written by
Jason Bittel

DK

DK | Penguin Random House

Illustrator Jonathan Woodward
Author Jason Bittel
Consultant Laure Cugnière
Project Editor Sophie Parkes
Senior Art Editor Claire Patane
Design Assistant Sif Nørskov
Editor Lizzie Munsey
US Editor Jane Perlmutter
US Senior Editor Shannon Beatty
Senior Designer Hannah Moore
Picture Researcher Rituraj Singh
Publishing Coordinator Issy Walsh
Senior Production Editor Dragana Puvacic
Senior Production Controller John Casey
Managing Editor Penny Smith
Deputy Art Director Mabel Chan
Publishing Director Sarah Larter

First American Edition, 2022
Published in the United States by DK Publishing
1745 Broadway, 20th Floor, New York, NY 10019

DK books are available at special discounts when purchased
in bulk for sales promotions, premiums, fund-raising, or educational
use. For details, contact: DK Publishing Special Markets,
1745 Broadway, 20th Floor, New York, NY 10019
SpecialSales@dk.com

Printed and bound in China

For the curious
www.dk.com

Contents

EXTINCT

REDISCOVERED

Introduction

When people in the past found a huge bone or pair of antlers in the ground, they took it as evidence that dragons and giants walked the Earth. We know now that these are fossils—traces of animals that lived long before us and are now extinct. It's important to know the history of the animals that have lived on Earth, so we can learn lessons and protect them in the future.

Fire-breathing dragons and monstrous giants aren't real. But you can find a terrifying, 10 ft long Komodo dragon with venom in its spit in Southeast Asia, and our oceans are home to the blue whale, which is bigger than every single dinosaur we know of.

My point? We are unbelievably lucky to share this planet with tons of fascinating, bizarre, and unique creatures. And the more we learn about them, the better chance we have of making sure they will still be around for generations to come.

Jason Bittel

Mass extinctions

The earth has seen **many extinctions** before. Most people know that a **giant asteroid** probably killed off the **dinosaurs**. But did you know that this is just **one of many apocalypses** to have taken place on this planet? In fact, the Earth has suffered **five mass extinctions** over the last 500 million years. All together, scientists believe these events wiped out 75 to 90 percent of all the species that have ever existed. Worst of all, many experts believe humans are now causing a **sixth mass extinction event**.

447 million years ago	383 million years ago	252 million years ago

ORDOVICIAN

The second-largest mass extinction in Earth's history seems to have had something to do with a massive, planet-wide ice age, followed by a great thaw. The event wiped out 85 percent of life on the planet—most of which had existed in the oceans.

LATE DEVONIAN

This mass extinction has been linked to climate change, which was possibly due to volcanic and asteroid events causing a drop in carbon dioxide in the atmosphere. Over the course of 20 million years or so, about 75 percent of life on Earth died out, much of it without leaving a trace.

PERMIAN-TRIASSIC

Known as the Great Dying, this event was caused by eruptions from a complex of volcanoes. Their eruptions caused a change in climate, causing ocean temperatures to skyrocket and forests to wither and die. Only four percent of ocean species survived, along with 25 percent of life on land.

Fossilized fern

Insect in amber

Trilobite fossil

Pterodactylus

Tyrannosaurus rex

Brown bear

Stegosaurus

Thylacine

Allosaurus

| 201 million years ago | 66 million years ago | Present day |

Huge volcanic eruptions in what is now the Atlantic Ocean seem to have fueled widespread climate change, causing this mass extinction event. The world's oceans probably became more acidic as a result, making it difficult for coral, snails, crabs, and other marine life to build their shells.

TRIASSIC-JURASSIC

The asteroid that caused this dinosaur-ending mass extinction is estimated to have been 7.4 mi (12 km) long when it hit modern-day Mexico's Yucatan Peninsula. The impact would have been unimaginable, vaporizing everything nearby, triggering wildfires for hundreds of miles, throwing the entire planet's climate completely out of whack.

CRETACEOUS-PALEOGENE

Scientists are very concerned about how quickly species are going extinct these days. In fact, many experts now agree humans have changed the Earth so much, so quickly, that we are now living in a new era. They call it the "Anthropocene," which comes from the Greek words for "human" and "new."

HOLOCENE

Triceratops skull

Ammonite fossil

Woolly mammoth

INVASIVE SPECIES

This is what we call species that have been brought to a new place by humans. Invasive species can drive native species to extinction by eating their food, taking their homes, and preying upon the native species or their young.

Harlequin ladybugs are invasive in North America and Europe.

HABITAT LOSS

Each species on Earth has evolved to live in a certain place. When that place's temperature, weather, and food supply are affected thanks to humans, many species disappear.

Crops are fertilized by chemicals that are damaging to wildlife.

EXPLOITATION

People exploit animals for all sorts of things. We eat them. We make clothing out of their skins and shells. We collect them to sell as pets, as decorations, or as traditional medicine products. Animals are also killed when they damage our crops and livestock.

Humans destroy animals' habitats, too, such as the gorilla's rainforest home.

POLLUTION

Oil spills, car exhaust, and plastic litter are just some of the many ways people mess up the environment. Pollution can sometimes poison animals immediately, or, in other cases, take decades to build up in their systems. Animals can choke on trash or get trapped in it and drown.

CLIMATE CHANGE

Small changes can stack up to have big impacts on wildlife. Climate change can reduce food supplies, make habitats disappear, and create conditions that species can no longer survive in.

Many factories burn materials and pump the dangerous waste gases out into the atmosphere.

Causes of extinction

You now know that life on Earth has suffered **many extinctions** in the past. But while death is natural, scientists say that what's happening now is different, because it has mostly been caused, and **can be prevented**, by humans. People are driving species to extinction much faster than would occur naturally, but if humans **change** their activity, they can **slow this process down**. Here are some of the **main reasons** it is happening so quickly at the moment.

Classification

Scientists have many different ways to track **how a species is doing**. They can study the **number of animals** that exist in the population of a particular species, or measure the **amount of habitat** that is left for those animals to live in. In this book, we'll focus on **four handy groupings**. What each of them means has been explained for you below.

EXTINCT

These species have disappeared forever. Some of the animals featured in this book became extinct before humans existed. Others have become history only recently.

Dodo

REDISCOVERED

Very rarely, scientists will spot an animal that was thought to have become extinct, or that was only known from fossils. Some call these critters zombie species, since they are "back from the dead."

Takahē

Pygmy tarsier

Javan rhinoceros

Giant panda

ENDANGERED

Endangered species are those that are threatened with extinction. This can result from overhunting or fishing, loss of habitat, climate change, or a number of other causes.

RECOVERING

These species are considered endangered, but they are no longer as close to extinction as they once were, thanks to the work of researchers and conservationists.

Bornean orangutan

California condor

Conservation

This world is **worth fighting for**. It's true that **we are to blame** for most of the extinctions happening today, but we also have the **power to stop them**. Some animals have **already been saved** from extinction: every time a humpback whale breaches or a bald eagle soars overhead, it's a reminder that it's **not too late** to save creatures under threat. **Conservation** is the word we use for protecting and caring for nature.

The pangolin is probably the most trafficked mammal on Earth. In 2016, world governments came together to make it illegal to buy and sell these animals.

REWILDING

Returning plant and animal species to places where they have disappeared from can help us rebuild the Earth's rich network of living things. Wild spaces are good for humans' mental health, too.

PROTECTED AREAS

Animals can't survive without their habitats. One of the best things we can do for animals is to protect the large areas of forests, reefs, prairies, wetlands, and everything in between, that they call home.

PREVENT CLIMATE CHANGE

This is a biggie, but the world needs to come together and cut down on the use of fossil fuels such as oil or coal, to stop climate change. Using cars less often is one way that you could help.

KEYSTONE SPECIES

These are animals that each ecosystem (community of wildlife) would fall apart without, such as bees. By identifying and protecting keystone species, we can protect the many other species that rely on them.

REDUCE, REUSE, RECYCLE

Small changes make a difference. Picking up litter can help animals nearby, while buying fewer clothes, plastics, and even smartphones can help everything from sea turtles to mountain gorillas.

Ecosystems

The ozone layer is a layer of gases high above Earth that protects Earth from dangerous rays from the sun.

It might be hard to understand why we need to save animals most of us will never see, but every **ecosystem** is like a **house**. The plants and animals that live there are the bricks that make up that house. Take one or two bricks away as animals become **extinct**, and the house will keep standing. But **eventually**, if you take away too many bricks, the whole thing **collapses**.

PLANTS

Plants convert sunlight into energy in a process called photosynthesis. They give off oxygen, which all animals need to breathe to survive.

All the things on this planet are tied to each

Only 2.5% of Earth's water is fresh—the rest is salty. We need to keep what we have clean, and protect our lakes and rivers.

OCEANS

Our oceans are amazing. They release oxygen and absorb carbon dioxide. They also take in heat and make sure it's spread evenly around the planet.

16

When everything is in balance, the Earth provides the perfect home for all living things. Every animal and plant has a part to play.

other—we are all connected!

ATMOSPHERE

The gases that are in the air are called atmosphere. They let the right amount of heat in and out of Earth. But the gases have to be in the perfect balance to work properly. If we put too much carbon dioxide into the atmosphere, the Earth will become too hot —this is what we call climate change.

Trees are Known as the lungs of the Earth, because they take in carbon dioxide and release oxygen.

ANIMALS

Animals breathe in oxygen and breathe out carbon dioxide, which plants use for photosynthesis. They also help plants by moving their seeds around and pollinating their flowers.

Plants also provide food and shelter for animals.

Saber-toothed cat

Smilodon fatalis

Talk about if looks could kill! The saber-toothed cat was a **gigantic predator**, weighing up to 600 lb (272 kg) and sporting 7 in (18 cm) long canine teeth, which it sunk deep into the bison, tapirs, and deer it hunted. It's **unclear** exactly why the saber-toothed cat became extinct, but it was probably due to there being fewer big animals to eat, climate change, and competition with other **aggressive-looking predators**.

SNEAK ATTACK

Saber-toothed cats are thought to have been ambush predators, relying on thick brush and woodlands to hide their colossal frames.

Smilodon fatalis means "deadly knife tooth."

IT'S A TRAP!

Over the years, scientists have unearthed around 166,000 saber-toothed cat bones at the La Brea Tar Pits in Los Angeles, US. The sabers and other predators apparently couldn't resist nibbling on animals that had become stuck in the thick, liquid tar, and eventually became victims to the sticky trap themselves.

The skull of a saber-toothed cat, featuring its huge, curved teeth

The skeleton of a saber-toothed cat

Sometimes called saber-toothed lions or tigers, Smilodon fatalis were actually not closely related to any modern kitties.

Despite its name, the Irish elk was not an elk, nor was it only found in Ireland. In fact, it was a deer, and ranged across much of Europe.

Irish elk antlers could weigh up to 90 lb (41 kg), making them the largest antlers ever recorded.

Irish elk

Megaloceros giganteus

The Irish elk was one of the **most massive deer** to ever live. The most likely reason for its extinction is climate change. Cooling temperatures may have reduced its food supply of grass, shoots, and leaves. Warming also seems to have changed the species' home from open grassland to thick forests. Without food to fuel their gigantic bodies, female elk would have given birth to fewer and fewer calves each year.

ANTLERS OF DOOM

Scientists used to think that the elk's antlers played a part in their downfall. They thought that they were so big and heavy that the deer would fall into bogs and get stuck in trees, causing them to die out. However, scientists don't believe that any more.

HOOD ORNAMENTS

Like modern elk, male Irish elk used their antlers to fight each other and compete for mates. Female Irish elk didn't have antlers.

Irish elk were last seen around 8,000 years ago.

Humans were on the rise at the time the Irish elk became extinct. It's possible that hunting may have pushed the elk, which was already rare, over the edge.

Giant ground sloth

Megatherium americanum

Sloths today spend most of their lives moving slowly through the treetops. Their ancestors, however, were **hulking, ground-walking giants**. One of the many species of ground sloth was *Megatherium*, an enormous creature with a 20 ft (6 m) long body, weighing nearly 4 tons (3.6 tonnes). In fact, scientists believe this sloth was one of the **largest land mammals** that ever existed.

While many people associate sloths with South America, ground sloth fossils have been found as far north as Alaska and the Canadian Yukon. Most ground sloths disappeared around **10,000 years ago**, after the end of the last ice age.

Sloths alive today are about the size of a small dog, but *Megatherium americanum* was closer to the size of an elephant.

Giant ground sloths were able to walk on their hind legs as they reached for food.

Large, curved tusks were probably used to fight and to remove snow and ice from grass and small plants before eating.

HAIRY HERBIVORE

This plant-eating giant was covered in layers of thick, shaggy hair that kept it warm in freezing conditions. Its distinctive hump stored energy, allowing it to survive for long periods of time without food.

Woolly mammoth

Mammuthus primigenius

The woolly mammoth is one of the most well-known animals of the Ice Age. This **lumbering giant** roamed icy grasslands of the Northern Hemisphere and was well-adapted to survive **freezing winters**. It lived on Earth for about five million years, and the last remaining group of mammoths became extinct about 3,700 years ago. At that time, **humans hunted them** for their meat and bones. Some scientists believe that humankind may have hunted them to extinction.

The woolly mammoth was still alive when the pyramids of Egypt were being built.

CLOSE RELATIVES
Scientists studied the DNA of frozen mammoths found in Siberia and found that it is remarkably similar to the DNA of today's Asian elephants.

HIPPOS IN HIDING?

The most recent Malagasy dwarf hippo
fossils appear to be about 1,000 years old,
but locals have described seeing animals
that fit the hippos' description during
modern times. Until proof can be found,
the species will remain classified as extinct.

Malagasy dwarf hippopotamus

Hippopotamus lemerlei

The African island of Madagascar has all kinds of wildlife found
nowhere else on Earth, including lemurs, tenrecs, and fossas. Until
recently, it also had **tiny hippos**! It's unclear how these animals made it
onto the island—it's possible that they swam across from mainland Africa,
when the ocean was lower and small chains of islands were present that
no longer exist. Whatever the case, dwarf hippos are the only hoofed
mammals ever known to have been native to Madagascar.

Knife marks on some Malagasy dwarf hippo fossils suggest that they were once hunted by humans.

Eyes placed high up on the hippos' skulls allowed them to see above the water.

It's thought that Malagasy dwarf hippos ate grass, and lived partly on land and partly in water.

The dodo would have been around 3 ft (1 m) tall.

Studies have shown that the dodo's brain size was average—another hint that these animals may not have been dummies after all.

The dodo couldn't fly—its wings helped it to balance.

Dodo

Raphus cucullatus

The dodo was a **large, flightless bird** native to the island of Mauritius in the Indian Ocean. It has a reputation for being slow and stupid because it foolishly lacked a fear of humans. Today's scientists, however, believe the dodo was a **strong, quite successful bird**. It only took a nosedive after humans started hunting it, cutting down its forests, and introducing non-native species such as pigs and rats.

In fact, you could argue that dodos were excellent survivors. They managed to stick around for **several million years** before becoming extinct, while humans have only been around for 200,000 years so far.

According to German zoologist Georg Wilhelm Steller, who this animal was named after, the sea cow's blubber tasted delightful, with a slight hint of almond.

SOCIAL ANIMALS

These animals were said to be highly social, and would even defend each other if they were attacked.

BIG-BONED

Dense, heavy bones may have helped these cold-water creatures balance out the floating caused by their thick blubber.

Steller's sea cow

Hydrodamalis gigas

Imagine a manatee **larger than an orca**, and you will start to understand what it was like to behold a Steller's sea cow. Unfortunately, imagination is all we have, because the species was hunted to extinction by hungry fur traders by 1768—just **27 years** after it was officially described.

ICE, ICE BABY

Steller's sea cows were cold-water specialists. They kept warm using their great size and thick blubber.

The Steller's sea cow is the first marine mammal known to have been driven to extinction by humans.

EXTINCT

Great auk beaks, feathers, and bones have been found in human burial sites from around 4,000 years ago. This suggests the birds were important to ancient peoples in some way.

Great auk

Pinguinus impennis

The great auk was like a penguin in many ways. Both birds sport **black-and-white feathers**, spend most of their lives at sea, and have wings too short for flying but **perfect for swimming**. One big difference? Penguins are found in the Southern Hemisphere, while the great auk lived in the North. Great auks became victims of **hungry sailors** desperate for fresh meat, as well as those who made money selling the birds' feathers, fat, oil, and eggs. Thanks to these practices, the curious, 3 ft (1 m) tall birds were driven to extinction in 1884, before scientists ever really even got a chance to study them.

Mottling on the great auk's eggs helped them blend in with rocks on the shore.

STRIPE HYPE

Scientists are still trying to figure out why zebras and quaggas evolved stripes. Working theories include stripes as camouflage from predators, as protection from biting flies, or as a way to cool down.

Quagga

Equus quagga quagga

With fewer stripes and a much browner color than the **zebra**, the quagga was originally thought to be its own species. Studies of DNA, however, showed that the quagga and zebra were **closely related**, so scientists decided to classify the quagga as a **subspecies** of the plains zebra (the most common type of zebra). The quagga was only known to exist in South Africa.

Hunting by European colonists in South Africa drove the quagga to extinction in the late 1800s.

ZEBRA HEAD, HORSE BUTT

From behind, you might have mistaken a quagga for a brown horse. Stripes on the front half, however, would have revealed the animal's true identity.

Like the zebra, the quagga was a grazer, feeding mostly on grasses.

THE QUAGGA PROJECT

Because quaggas and plains zebras are so closely related, some scientists are trying to bring quaggas back from extinction. By selecting plains zebras with fewer and fewer stripes on their haunches to breed together, the Quagga Project has successfully started to breed animals that look like quaggas.

There are three species of zebra alive today, and each has slightly different stripe patterns. The plains zebra is the most common.

The Grevy's zebra has cone-shaped ears, like those of a mule, with a white belly.

The mountain zebra looks like a cross between the other two species, but with an orange snout.

Passenger pigeon

Ectopistes migratorius

In the early 1800s, there were around three billion passenger pigeons in North America, making the species the **most common bird on the continent.** So, what happened? Well, the birds were apparently quite tasty, and pioneers killed many of them to get **fresh protein** to eat. Probably the bigger problem, however, was that these birds could gobble down an **entire crop harvest** in just a few days. So, people started poisoning the flocks, catching them with nets and burning down their roost trees.

SAFETY IN NUMBERS

Passenger pigeons would fly and roost in enormous flocks, sometimes made up of millions of birds. Having a lot of other birds around is thought to have helped them thrive. There was no way a hawk, owl, or coyote could eat all of them!

When passenger pigeon flocks flew overhead, they were so thick they could block out the sun, and could take hours to pass over a single spot.

LAST OF HER KIND
The last passenger pigeon on
Earth was named Martha. She
died at the Cincinnati Zoo in
the US, on September 1, 1914.

So many passenger
pigeons would nest in a single
tree that the branches broke
under their weight.

Female thylacines would carry
two to four young in a backward-facing
pouch on their belly.

ISLAND LIVING

Thylacines used to be
native to mainland Australia,
as well as to the islands of
Tasmania and New Guinea.

Thylacine

Thylacinus cynocephalus

With the stripes of a tiger, the body of a wolf, and the pouch of a kangaroo, the thylacine was a fascinating creature, which still puzzles scientists today. Also known as the Tasmanian tiger, it was a **meat-eating marsupial**, most closely related to Tasmanian devils and numbats. The last known thylacine, named **Benjamin**, died on September 7, 1936. Since then, there have been rumors of thylacine sightings, but **no evidence**.

The thylacine's stripes are thought to have helped it sneak through the dark underbrush after its prey, which was mostly birds and small possums.

DOG FIGHT

Some scientists believe that competition with the dingo, Australia's wild dog, led to the thylacine's demise. Hunting by humans may have also played a role.

Believe it or not, there is one place you can still see the thylacine—on the internet! A short video clip from 1933 shows Benjamin pacing around his enclosure. The film is haunting, since it shows the very last thylacine Known to exist.

The last known wild crescent nail-tail wallaby was caught in a trap set for dingoes (Australian wild dogs) in 1928.

Like other marsupials, wallabies nurse their young in pouches until they're big enough to hop.

Crescent nail-tail wallaby

Onychogalea lunatad

Most people have heard of kangaroos, but did you know there are many species of smaller, kangaroo-like marsupials called **wallabies**? The crescent nail-tail wallaby was one of them, named after the tiny, clawlike tip on its tail.

Common across central, southern, and southwestern Australia before it was colonized by Europeans, this species **couldn't adapt quickly enough** to the changes happening on its continent. This is because the Europeans brought other animals with them, such as foxes and cats, which preyed upon the wallabies and their young. Non-native rabbits and cattle also **chowed down on the grasses** that the nail-tails needed to survive.

Golden toad

Incilicus periglenes

The mysterious golden toad was once an abundant species native to Monteverde Cloud Forest, Costa Rica. But in 2004 this vibrant amphibian was declared extinct and experts still debate the cause. One theory is that changes in climate led to an unusually hot, dry season that affected the golden toad's two-and-a-half-square-mile habitat. It was also vulnerable to a disease, called Chytridiomycosis, which flourished in warmer regions and led to a decline in similar groups of amphibians.

ONE OF A KIND

In 1972, scientists observed around 1,500 golden toads in Monteverde Cloud Forest, but by 1988 this had fallen to ten. In May 1989, they recorded just one lone male—the last golden toad to ever be seen.

The extinction of the golden toad was the first to be blamed on global warming as a result of human activity, but recent evidence suggests human activity may not be to blame.

OUT OF SIGHT

Golden toads spent most of
their lives in underground
burrows beneath the damp
forest floor. In the rainy
season they would emerge to
breed in puddles and ponds.

Twenty species of frogs
and toads went extinct
in the same region and
at a similar time to
the golden toad.

SENSITIVE SKIN

Like other amphibians, the
golden toad had thin skin that
helped it to absorb oxygen and
breathe, but that may have
made it more vulnerable to
pollution and toxins.

43

Pinta Island tortoise

Chelonoidis abingdonii

It's not often that you can pin down the extinction of an entire species to a **single moment**, but for the Pinta Island tortoise, that day was June 24, 2012. This is when the last known Pinta Island tortoise on earth died. His name was **Lonesome George**, and he was about 100 years old.

Since 1972, George had lived at the Charles Darwin Research Station on the **Galápagos Islands**, where scientists tried many times to breed him with other giant tortoise species. The babies produced from such a pair wouldn't have been 100 percent Pinta Island tortoise, but the hope was to save at least some of George's genes from extinction. Unfortunately, none of the breeding efforts resulted in turtle hatchlings.

Many species of giant
tortoise still live on islands,
such as Ecuador's Galápagos
Islands and the Seychelles in
the Indian Ocean.

Pinta Island tortoise
numbers declined as
sailors and whalers
hunted the animals
for their meat.

LOOK OUT BELOW!

Flying squirrels don't actually fly. Instead, they glide through the air, using flaps of skin called patagia that stretch between their limbs.

This species was named for the thick, wool-like fur on its bushy tail.

POTTY TALK

Woolly flying squirrels often live in caves, cliffs, and rock crevices, where their feces and urine build up into a sticky, piney goo. Some people believe this goo has medicinal properties.

In 2021, scientists figured out that there isn't just one species of woolly flying squirrel—there are three!

Woolly flying squirrels are one of the few animals that eat mostly pine needles.

Woolly flying squirrel

Eupetaurus cinereus

What's four feet long, weighs as much as a chihuahua, and can glide through the sky on wings made of skin and fluff? The woolly flying squirrel, one of the largest gliding rodents on Earth! In 1888, the species was described from several skins and one skull. Then these critters went into hiding for nearly 100 years, until they were rediscovered by scientists in Pakistan, in 1994. The species is now considered to be endangered.

At one point in history, there were about 90 different species of coelacanth. Today, just two species remain. At least, as far as we know!

The tail is flat and powerful, allowing the fish to thrust forward at great speed.

DEEP WATER

Both coelacanth species live far below the ocean's surface, in water so deep that light from the sun starts to fizzle out. Scientists call this place the Twilight Zone.

Coelacanth

Genus latimeria

Scientists thought the fish known as the coelacanth became extinct around the same **time as the dinosaurs**. But then, in 1938, a museum curator discovered one of these toothy beasts in a fisherman's haul in South Africa. What's more, a **second species**, the Indonesian coelacanth, was discovered off the coast of the island of Sulawesi, Indonesia, in 1997.

A coelacanth can grow up to 6.5 ft (1.9 m) in length and weigh nearly 200 lb (91 kg).

The fish can open its mouth very wide to catch prey such as fish, octopus, and squid.

EXTINCT?

Before rediscovery, coelacanths were only known from fossils dating back 65 million years. Some now call the fish "living fossils," because they are a species which has hardly changed in millions of years.

A coelacanth fossil

A TALE OF TWO FISHES

The two living species of coelacanth look fairly similar, but DNA tests show that they are actually quite different. This suggests the two species have been separated for several millions of years.

The Indonesian coelacanth

Tree lobster

Dryococelus australis

The tree lobster is one of the **largest insects in the world**. Originally, it had only been found on **Lord Howe Island**, Australia. The species was declared extinct in 1983, because it hadn't been seen for decades.

In 1960, however, a group of climbers visited a nearby sea stack known as **Ball's Pyramid**, and found evidence that tree lobsters might live there, too. This was confirmed in 2001, when scientists found a small population of tree lobsters in a **tea tree on a cliff**, high above the ocean. DNA tests revealed that they were of the same species, meaning the magnificent creatures hadn't disappeared after all. They are now being reintroduced to Lord Howe Island.

A shipwreck in 1918 accidentally unleashed black rats onto Lord Howe Island. The rats devoured the juicy tree lobsters, as well as several other species of birds and insects.

AN UGLY MUG

This species is known for the long, flowing, reddish-tinged fins of its males. It also has a grimacing face, similar to that of a gargoyle.

Mangarahara cichlid

Ptychochromis insolitus

What good is a fish **without water**? This is the danger for the Mangarahara cichlid, a fish native to a **small stretch of river** in Madagascar. Much of the water from this fish's home was used up by rice farming, leaving its habitat **so dry** in places that the fish was **assumed to be extinct** in the wild. Luckily, a Malagasy man knew of a group of them living in a small pool of water. In 2013, he led a group of experts there, who moved them to tanks where they could breed in safety Today, the species is still in danger, but hanging on, thanks to **captive breeding** programs in Madagascar and Canada.

Part of this fish's scientific name, "insolitus," means "unusual" —because of the weird, comblike structures on its scales.

MOTHER KNOWS BEST

The female Mangarahara cichlids protect their eggs, but in some other species of cichlid, the males take care of the young.

Scientists hope to eventually relocate the Mangarahara cichlid to a protected area near its original home.

LIFE IN THE TREETOPS

Pygmy tarsiers live high up in the mountainous cloud forests (tropical forests that get heavy rain and lots of clouds) of Sulawesi, Indonesia. They are nocturnal and eat insects, spiders, and other arthropods.

Cloud forests are found very high up in the mountains.

Pygmy tarsiers can't move their gigantic eyes. They can look around, however, by rotating their necks 180°, like owls.

Baby pygmy tarsiers can climb trees within a day of being born.

Tarsiers are quite weird, as primates go! They have claws instead of fingernails.

Pygmy tarsier

Tarsius pumilus

Did you know you have a relative the size of a **small mouse**? That's right—pygmy tarsiers are **prosimian primates**, which are more closely related to humans than monkeys. Each one could **fit in your pocket** and weighs about as much as **two slices of bread**. Don't underestimate these tiny creatures, though. After researchers found the first pygmy tarsiers seen alive since the 1920s, one of them took a **bite** out of a researcher's finger as she tried to put a tracking collar on it. Ouch!

The tarsier is named after its extra-long ankle bone, the tarsus.

THREATS

Today, the pygmy tarsier is classified as endangered, because its populations are small and far apart. Logging and the increasing presence of humans are also threats to its survival.

The Bermuda petrel has another name, cahow, which mimics the sound of its call.

Bermuda petrels can drink seawater, thanks to a special gland (type of organ) that helps them filter salt and then sneeze it out. Achoo!

Bermuda petrel

Pterodroma cahow

For **hundreds of years**, people thought the Bermuda petrel had become extinct. You see, throughout the 1500s and 1600s, Spanish and English sailors ate the birds voraciously. They also released feral hogs—pigs that had a taste for petrel eggs. Then, in 1951, the species was rediscovered, nesting in a **series of rocky inlets**. There were only 17 nesting pairs, so conservationists had to work quickly, relocating some of the birds to a protected island nearby called **Nonsuch**. The experts even dug **artificial burrows** for the tunnel-digging birds, to help them get started. Today, there are more than 100 nesting pairs of Bermuda petrels. Though that's a long way off from the half-million that existed before, it gives the species a **fighting chance** of survival.

HOT TO TROT

Chacoan peccaries are native to the hot and dry regions of Paraguay, Bolivia, and Argentina in South America, where they eat cacti. A cactus must be de-spined first, so they pull out the prickles with their teeth and spit them out.

Tiny hooves allow peccaries to tiptoe through thorny underbrush.

VANISHING WORLD

Chacoan peccaries are listed as endangered, because their habitat is disappearing. Only a few thousand remain—their home has been converted into cattle ranches, oil platforms, and roads.

Chacoan peccary

Catagonus wagneri

These days, discovering a **new species of large mammal** is pretty rare. So, the Chacoan peccary was big news when it first plodded onto the scene in 1975. That is, until other scientists said, "Wait a minute! We know this animal, but from old fossils. This thing is supposed to be extinct." Surprise! The Chacoan peccary had been **hiding out in the scrub** all along.

Though peccaries and pigs look similar, they last shared a common ancestor about 40 million years ago. They also have different teeth, toes, and tails.

The name of the bird originates from the Māori word takahi, which means "to trample."

TAKAHĒ COMEBACK

Conservation efforts have included taking eggs from the wild and raising them with puppets that look like the adult birds. This stops the chicks from becoming attached to their human keepers.

Takahē can live for between 16 and 18 years in the wild.

These birds may look pretty, but their sharp, red beaks pack a powerful bite!

ROAD TO RECOVERY

Thanks to the hard work of scientists and conservationists, there are now more than 400 takahē.

Takahē

Porphyrio hochstetteri

The takahē is a flightless bird **native to New Zealand's South Island**. The species was thought to be extinct for about 50 years, until it was **rediscovered in a remote valley** in the **Murchison Mountains** in 1948. Scientists believe a combination of climate change, competition with non-native red deer for grass, and death by non-native stoats are what put the species in trouble. Some of these threats continue. In 2007, for example, a **plague** of meat-eating least weasels cut the recovering population of takahē in half.

The crested gecko is also known as the eyelash gecko, because of the hairlike spines that run from its eyebrows to its tail.

HEADS OR TAILS?

Crested geckos can detach their tails to fool or confuse predators. Unlike other reptiles, however, their tails don't grow back.

Crested gecko

Correlophus ciliatus

The crested gecko is a reptile that lives in the **treetops** of New Caledonia, an island near Australia. Cresties are arboreal (tree-living) specialists. They have **tails that can grab hold** of branches, and **hairlike structures** on their footpads that allow them to stick to nearly any surface—even glass!

Crested geckos are also **common pets**, which is strange, since the species was thought to be extinct until it was spotted in the wild in 1994. At that time, scientists brought a few of the animals into **captivity**, where they made tons of babies. They remain **rare** in their natural home, thanks to invasive species such as fire ants, rats, and cats.

The Leadbeater's possum is the official mammal of the Australian state of Victoria.

HARD TO KNOW

Being tiny, nocturnal, and fast as lightning makes the Leadbeater's possum tough to keep tabs on. Scientists, however, say that there may be fewer than 1,500 of these animals left.

Leadbeater's possum

Gymnobelideus leadbeateri

Once thought to be extinct, today, Leadbeater's possums are considered **critically endangered** due to not having many places to live any more. These tiny, squirrel-like marsupials live in **trees** and nest in holes. They eat the sugary **sap** that leaks out of trees, as well as spiders, crickets, beetles, and other **invertebrates** that live on tree bark. All of those things are in short supply these days, having been destroyed by logging and forest fires.

In the Leadbeater's possum world, Mom is in charge. Scientists call this a matriarchal society.

POSSUM OR OPOSSUM?

They sound similar, but one little letter can make a big difference.

"Possum" refers to a suborder of tree-climbing mammals that live in Australia, New Guinea, and Sulawesi.

"Opossum" refers to the Virginia opossum and its cousins in North and South America.

Both possums and opossums (such as the one above) are marsupials—mammals that raise their young in a pouch. Kangaroos and koalas are both marsupials.

The Bulmer's fruit bat has only been found roosting in one cave, known as Luplupwintem, in Papua New Guinea.

GO FIGURE

As its name suggests, this bat species is thought to eat mostly fruit, including figs.

Bulmer's fruit bat

Aproteles bulmerae

So far, the Bulmer's fruit bat has risen from the dead **twice**! First, scientists believed the species died out at the end of the last ice age. Then, in the 1970s, the bats were discovered in a **cave** in Papua New Guinea. Return visits to the cave came up empty until, in 1992, an expedition revealed more than **100 bats**. There are even signs that the colony is **growing**! The species is considered critically endangered.

With its wings fully open, the Bulmer's fruit bat is 3 ft (1 m) wide! It is the largest cave-roosting bat in the world.

Despite its size, the Bulmer's fruit bat is extremely agile. Unusually for a bat, it can fly backward and hover.

The red-crested tree-rat's tail can stretch nearly 11 in (28 cm) long and ends in grayish-white fluff.

The red-crested tree-rat is nocturnal.

Before 2011, the red-crested tree-rat hadn't been seen for nearly a century!

SECRETS, SECRETS

Scientists know almost nothing about red-crested tree-rats, including how many are left, how they reproduce, and even what they eat.

Red-crested tree-rat

Santamartamys rufodorsalis

The red-crested tree-rat is a **gerbil-sized** critter that's only been seen by scientists a grand total of **three times**! The most recent sighting came in 2011, from two volunteers at a nature reserve in northern Colombia. They were about to go to bed when this rusty-red rodent crawled up the steps of their lodge and sat there for nearly **two hours**. The species is considered critically endangered.

Asian elephant

Elephas maximus

Native to India and Southeast Asia, this elephant is slightly **smaller** than its African cousin, but still the **largest land animal** on its continent. Both kinds of elephants live in **female-led** family groups. Young males form their own groups, while older, dominant males tend to go it alone.

Small, rounded ears are one way to identify an Asian elephant.

With 20,000 to 40,000 Asian elephants left, this species is endangered.

African elephant

Loxodonta sp.

African elephants inhabit the African continent. These giants are **smart**, and can communicate over large distances using low, vibrating rumbles. **Habitat loss** and **poaching** remain the largest threats for these creatures, since there is still great demand for the **ivory** that makes up their **tusks**.

Large ears help them get rid of extra heat, so they can cool off.

There are two species of African elephant: the bush elephant and the smaller forest elephant.

The bears regularly swim up to 30 miles (48 km) at a time. One bear paddled more than 220 miles (354 km) across open ocean!

WORLD OF ICE

Polar bears rely on sea ice for their survival—it's where they hunt, mate, build dens, and give birth.

Polar bear

Ursus maritimus

Everything about the polar bear is built for a **life in the cold**. Huge, furry paw pads insulate the bears from freezing temperatures while doubling as snowshoes. White fur camouflages the animals from the seals they hunt, while black skin absorbs heat from the sun. The trouble is, as **climate change** reduces the amount of ice found in the Arctic, the polar bear's world is changing probably faster than it can adapt.

Climate change is already visible in the Arctic. Sea ice takes longer to form in the fall and melts earlier in the spring because the temperature is getting warmer.

HUNTING FOR FOOD

Polar bears are the most carnivorous bears on Earth. They survive mostly on seals, which they catch as the seals come up to the water's surface for air.

Polar bears can swim at a pace of about 6 mph (9.9 km/h), which is faster than human Olympians!

The rhino's large, curved tusks were probably used to fight and remove snow and ice from grass and small plants before eating.

Javan rhino

Rhinoceros sondaicus

The magnificent Javan rhino had long been hunted for its horn. Today, it has almost been hunted to extinction and is considered critically endangered. The only remaining Javan rhinos can be found in Indonesia's Ujung Kulon National Park in **West Java**, where steps are being taken to save this spectacular species from extinction.

With fewer than 70 left on Earth, the Javan rhino is one the rarest large mammals in the world.

WORKING TOGETHER

The International Rhino Foundation has employed people to remove invasive palms and encourage the growth of rhino-friendly plants in an area of the **Ujung Kulon National Park**. This has led to increased numbers of Javan rhinos and higher employment in the local community.

SPECIES OF RHINO

There are five types of rhino, each with unique quirks and characteristics.

Conservationists have helped grow Indian rhino populations from 200 to 2,700.

White rhino populations recovered from just 100 in 1985, to more than 18,000 today.

After huge declines in black rhinos in the 1970's, there are now more than 5,000.

The Sumatran rhino has survived on Earth longer than any other living mammal, but there are fewer than 80 left in the wild.

Leatherbacks are found all across the world's oceans. Some populations, however, are declining quickly, and the species is considered vulnerable to extinction.

A leatherback turtle can hold its breath for 85 minutes!

Leatherback turtle

Dermochelys coriacea

Not only is the leatherback the world's chunkiest turtle, but it is also the **largest noncrocodilian reptile** on planet Earth. Fully-grown adults can tip the scales at about 2,000 lb (907 kg), which is nearly 15 times the weight of an average adult human. This is also the only turtle with a **flexible, rubbery shell** covered in skin. Scientists believe this helps it travel more quickly through the water.

Leatherback sea turtles
are like submarines, capable
of diving to depths of
4,200 ft (1,280 m).

JELLY TIME
The leatherback's favorite
food is jellyfish. It has
backward-facing spines in
its throat, which help slurp
down this slimy prey.

Eastern mountain gorilla

Gorilla beringei

Native to the Democratic Republic of the Congo, Uganda, and Rwanda, the two subspecies of eastern gorilla are both considered **critically endangered**. As few as 2,600 of these great apes now remain. Poaching, climate change, and clearing forests for agriculture are the eastern gorilla's **greatest threats**.

Eastern gorillas are the largest primates in the world.

Troops of eastern gorillas can include up to 30 animals.

Western gorilla

Gorilla gorilla

With a population of nearly 100,000, western gorillas are in **better shape** than their cousins to the east. The two western gorilla subspecies, however, are also **critically endangered** due to poaching, habitat loss, and climate change. The animals are also threatened by human diseases, such as the Ebola virus.

Western gorillas are smaller and lighter in color than eastern gorillas.

Western gorillas are the only gorillas known to use tools.

Queen Alexandra's birdwing

Ornithoptera alexandrae

With its wings opened wide, the Queen Alexandra's birdwing is easily **larger than your face**. Interestingly, males and females of this species look **completely different**. Both are huge, but females tend to be larger, with brown and tan coloring. Males are smaller but more **brightly colored**—they have a yellow abdomen (belly) and neon green, blue, and black wings.

Queen Alexandra's birdwings only exist on the eastern half of **New Guinea**, a large island just north of Australia. Scientists believe they rely on large, old forests, where they fly high up in the tree canopy. **Logging** is the biggest reason for the species' endangered status—without forests, they can't complete their life cycle. Much of their habitat was also destroyed by a **volcanic eruption** in 1951.

Unlike many insects, these butterflies only lay up to 30 eggs at a time. This slow reproduction rate makes it harder for them to bounce back.

Amur leopard

Panthera pardus orientalis

Leopards aren't just found in Africa. In fact, the subspecies known as the Amur leopard is native to **parts of Russia and China**, near the Amur River. **Just over 100** of these kitties, however, remain. Amur leopards are threatened by poaching for their lovely, cream-colored coats, loss of prey for them to eat, and habitat destruction.

LEAPING LEOPARDS

Amur leopards can spring 10 ft (3 m) up into the air from standing, and jump up to 19 ft (5.8 m) along the ground— more than twice the human long jump record.

The Amur leopard is probably the world's rarest big cat.

ROOM FOR HOPE

In 2007, there were only 30 Amur leopards left. Efforts to save these cats have helped their population more than triple since.

Amur Leopards are top predators, and can take down deer or boar nearly three times their size.

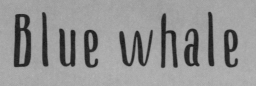

Blue whale

Balaenoptera musculus

Nothing in the history of this planet has ever grown as huge as the blue whale—not even the dinosaurs! In fact, the blue whale is **so colossal** that its tongue weighs as much as an elephant and its heart could balance a scale with a car. Surprisingly, these gargantuan creatures put on pounds by gobbling up clouds of **tiny, shrimplike krill**.

BIG THREAT
Even the world's largest animal sometimes falls victim to predators such as orcas and sharks. Unrestricted hunting by humans between 1900 and the 1960s led to the blue whale becoming endangered.

Blue whales can be found in every ocean on Earth, except the Arctic.

Blue whales are now protected, meaning that populations are slowly growing again. Fishing nets and boat collisions, however, still put the species in danger.

Blue whales use their 20 ft (6 m) wide tail, called a fluke, to push themselves through the water.

With lifespans similar to humans, blue whales can live for 80 to 90 years.

BIG BLUE

The pattern of blue-gray mottling on a blue whale's side is unique to each whale. Scientists can use these markings to tell individuals apart from each other over the years.

The humphead wrasse is one of the largest reef fish in the world.

A ROYAL CURSE

Some Asian and Oceanic cultures once considered humphead wrasse a delicacy fit only for royalty. More recently, regular people with enough money have decided they want to eat the fish, too. This rise in demand is the main reason the species is now classified as endangered.

Humphead wrasse

Cheilinus undulatus

At 400 lb (181 kg) and 6 ft (1.8 m) in length, the humphead wrasse is the size of a black bear. No wonder some call these fish the **kings of the coral reef**! What's perhaps most interesting about these animals is that they can sometimes **change sex—** from female to male. Scientists are still trying to figure out what prompts the transformation.

Males develop bigger, bluer humps on their foreheads as they age.

SERIOUS CHOMPERS

Humphead wrasse have two sets of teeth. The first is fused into a sharp beak, but the second set, called pharyngeal teeth, is found in the wrasse's throat. This helps the fish crunch down on mollusks, sea urchins, and crustaceans.

These blue-green behemoths can be found in coral reefs throughout the Indo-Pacific region.

CAN'T SEE ME

The red panda's color pattern is thought to help it blend in with reddish-brown moss and white lichen in the forest canopy.

Red pandas use their long, furry tails to help them balance in the treetops. This supersoft tail can also wrap around their bodies on cold nights, like a scarf.

Red panda

Ailurus fulgens

The red panda is an **impossibly cute**, fluffy, cat-sized native to **Asia**. Despite markings that make it look like a giant panda, red pandas are **not closely related** to the black-and-white bamboo eaters, but to a group of mammals that includes raccoons, weasels, and skunks.

Red Pandas can be found in China, Nepal, India, Myanmar, and Bhutan.

FADING FORESTS

Red pandas depend on healthy forests for their habitat, as well as their food. They are endangered due to deforestation across their range.

Like other penguins, the Galápagos penguin cannot fly, but swims through the ocean in search of small fish such as sardines, mullet, and anchovies.

Bare patches of skin on their cheeks help these birds shed heat.

Galápagos penguin

Spheniscus mendiculus

Did you know that not all penguins live in **Antarctica**? In fact, the Galápagos penguin is the northernmost penguin species. Part of its population lives in the **Galápagos Islands** of Ecuador, near the equator. Their small bodies, about 20 in (50 cm) tall, help these unusual penguins stay cool, while **caves** allow them to **hide** from the hot, tropical sun.

Galápagos penguins can pant like a dog, in order to cool off in the heat.

The Komodo dragon is the national animal of Indonesia. Indonesia is also the only country where these animals exist.

Komodo dragon

Varanus komodoensis

Meet the largest lizard on Earth, the Komodo dragon. These **real-life monster reptiles** may not be able to breathe fire, but they do grow up to 10 ft (3 m) in length and can weigh more than 300 lb (136 kg). Oh, and they have **venom glands** in their mouths that help with killing prey, such as the deer and water buffaloes found in their native habitat: Indonesia's Lesser Sunda Islands. Sometimes, they even eat **other dragons**.

The Komodo dragon used to be considered **Vulnerable** to extinction. In 2021, however, the species was given the more worrisome status of **endangered**. This is because the animals **only exist on islands**, and scientists predict that climate change and sea level rises will reduce the lizards' habitat by about one-third over the next 45 years.

Sensors in the snout act like a super sense, telling the gharial when fish swim near.

Gharials have the largest eggs of any crocodilian—each one can weigh 6 oz (170 g).

Gharial

Gavialis gangeticus

With a face like a pair of **needle-nose pliers**, the gharial is easily the **goofiest** crocodilian on the planet. It's also one of the **biggest**! At full size, male gharials can weigh about 2,200 lb (998 kg) and grow up to 20 ft (6 m) long. Despite its hugeness, the gharial nearly became extinct in the 1970s and is still listed as critically endangered. **Fewer than 250** of these fascinating reptiles are thought to remain today.

Male gharials grow bulbs of flesh on the tips of their noses that allow them to blow bubbles and make mating calls.

Gharials are expert swimmers, but they have weak legs. On land, they scoot on their bellies instead of walking.

NAMED AFTER ITS NOSE
The gharial's nose bulb is called a ghara, which is the Hindi word for a pot of a similar shape.

Bornean orangutan

Pongo pygmaeus

The word "orangutan" comes from the Malay language, where it means "forest person." This ape spends most of its time in trees, foraging for figs, mangos, ants, and leaves. The rapid disappearance of its forest habitat has put this species in danger—it is currently listed as critically endangered.

Orangutans are the only great apes found outside of Africa.

FOREST WISDOM

Orangutans pass knowledge down to their children, including how to use sticks and rocks as tools.

Female orangutans only give birth every 6 to 8 years.

Orangutans are the largest arboreal (tree-living) mammals on Earth.

Sunda pangolin

Manis javanica

Cross an anteater with a pineapple and what do you get? A pangolin! The Sunda pangolin is a species of pangolin found across Southeast Asia. All pangolins are covered in hard, overlapping scales made out of keratin—the same material as our hair and fingernails—which protect them from predators. Sadly, some people also believe pangolin scales can be used as medicine, so they poach the animals in great numbers.

Female Sunda pangolins give birth to one pup at a time.

Philippine pangolin

Manis culionensis

With a high demand for their scales, all pangolin species are in serious danger of extinction. But experts say the Philippine pangolin has a better chance of bouncing back than most. And the thanks for this goes to the people of the Philippines, who really want to save this species and who have been helping scientists learn more about the hard-to-study animals.

There are eight species of pangolin—four in Asia and four in Africa.

Some pangolin species use their tails to help them climb.

BIRDS OF A FEATHER

Bald eagles mate for life. Both parents take turns incubating their eggs and feeding the chicks fish, waterbirds, and other small animals.

White head feathers earned these birds their name, but they don't always look this way. Young eagles have brown head feathers until they are around five.

TREETOP MANSIONS

The largest bald eagle nest on record was 9.5 ft (2.9 m) across and 20 ft (6.1 m) tall. That's bigger than a full-grown giraffe!

Bald eagle

Haliaeetus leucocephalus

The bald eagle is one of the biggest birds in North America, yet these **white-headed predators** nearly disappeared last century. One big reason—people had just started using a pesticide known as **DDT**. This was good at killing bugs, but it was bad for birds because it **thinned out their eggshells,** making them more likely to crack.

By 1963, so many bald eagles had sat on and squashed their weak-shelled eggs that only **417 nesting pairs** remained in the continental US. People were able to save the baldies from extinction by banning DDT and protecting the species.

VEG HEAD

Pandas eat more plants than any other species of bear, surviving on a diet of mostly bamboo. They can eat up to 84 lb (38 kg) of the green stuff in a day.

Giant panda

Ailuropoda melanoleuca

MARATHON EATERS

Bamboo is low in nutrients, which means the bears need to eat lots of it. A giant panda can spend up to 19 hours eating each day.

Everybody loves the giant panda. They're huge, fluffy, black-and-white, and considered to be **gentle giants**. (But don't try to pet one. They're still bears, and as such have sharp teeth and large muscles designed to do **bear-sized damage**.) With just 1,000 or fewer animals left in the wild, the giant panda is considered **vulnerable** to extinction. China has recently made many important strides in protecting these animals, but giant panda populations still suffer from the effects of having their **forests cut down** in the past.

An extra "pseudo thumb" helps giant pandas grip long bamboo stems. It is actually part of their wrist bone.

Pandas are only found in South Central China.

ANCIENT ARTISTS

Humans have been aware of European bison for a long time. Cave art from 10,000 to 17,000 years ago seems to feature these big, brown beasts.

European bison

Bison bonasus

In 1924, no one thought the European bison would make it to the end of the century. The animals had been **hunted for food** for hundreds of years, until just 54 animals remained—and all of them lived in zoos. After decades of **captive breeding** and **releases back into the wild**, however, Europe's largest land mammal is back. There is now a population of around 7,000 animals, with the biggest herds in Poland, Belarus, and Russia.

European bison have fur that is less shaggy than that of their North American cousins.

LOCKED HORNS

When two male bison want to see who is most powerful, they engage in ritualized combat. This means they make a show of fighting, but they don't actually intend to hurt each other. To us, it just looks like they're banging their heads together.

European bison are a keystone species—they turn forests into grassland, spread seeds and nutrients in their dung, and provide food for predators and scavengers.

RECOVERING

ROAD TO RECOVERY

Burmese star tortoises nearly became extinct at the beginning of this century.

To save them, scientists took 175 tortoises to sanctuaries, where they could reproduce safely.

Now, more than 1,000 Burmese star tortoises have been returned to the wild.

Captive breeding efforts continue to produce several thousand Burmese star tortoise hatchlings each year.

Burmese star tortoise

Geochelone platynota

The Burmese star tortoise has a shell that looks like a **work of art**. Scientists say the beautiful designs help these slow-moving tortoises stay hidden among **grasses**. Grasses are common in the dry central region of **Myanmar**, a country in Southeast Asia. Myanmar was known as **Burma** until 1989. It is the only country in which the Burmese star tortoise can be found.

SEEING STARS?

Unfortunately, the tortoise's unique shell pattern makes it a favorite among collectors in the exotic pet trade. People also harvest the animals for their meat. Despite these challenges, the tortoise is recovering.

These soccer-ball-sized tortoises lift their shells completely off of the ground when they walk.

Baby humpbacks are called calves. They can be 15 ft (4.6 m) long at birth and drink 158 gal (600 l) of milk every day.

Humpback whale

Megaptera novaeangliae

The humpback can grow longer than a **school bus** and weigh up to 40 tons (36 tonnes). Several hundred years of large-scale **whaling** (hunting of whales), however, drove humpbacks and many other whale species to the edge. Fortunately, many countries came together to **ban** this kind of whaling in 1985, and humpback populations have now **increased**.

WHALES ON THE MOVE
Some humpback populations migrate thousands of miles each year, swimming between warm-water breeding grounds and cold-water feeding areas.

BIG WHALES, BIG PROBLEMS
The two biggest threats to humpbacks today are being hit by boats and getting tangled up in fishing gear.

Humpback whales are filter feeders, which means they use bristles called baleen to catch small fish and tiny crustaceans known as krill.

Iberian lynx

Lynx pardinus

The Iberian lynx is a wild cat, with a coat covered in black spots, a short, black tail, and **pointy tufts** of fur on its cheeks that make it look like it has a **beard**. The species is most closely related to the Eurasian lynx, but is only half its size. Iberian lynx depend on a healthy supply of **rabbits** to eat. When a virus killed off huge numbers of rabbits in the 1950s, the predators nearly disappeared with their prey.

As recently as 2002, there were **fewer than 100** Iberian lynx left. Scientists took some of the last cats into captivity and set up a **breeding program**. Today, **more than 1,000** of the secretive cats now prowl the mountains of Portugal and Spain.

THREATS OLD AND NEW

California condors are scavengers—
they eat the carcasses of animals that
are already dead. They can easily be
harmed by poisons in their food, such
as a now-banned pesticide called
DDT and lead from hunting bullets.

A bald head may help condors
avoid getting nasty stuff in
their feathers while eating
rotting meat.

Sharp, strong beaks
allow condors to tear
flesh and break bones.

Using rising currents of warm air, California condors fly as high as 15,000 ft (4,570 m) above the ground.

California condor

Gymnogyps californianus

The California condor soars through the air on 10 ft (3 m) wide wings—the **largest wingspan** of all North American birds. In 1987, the entire population of these condors dipped down to just **27 birds**. Scientists brought all of them into captivity where they could help them breed, and today there are more than **300**. Much work is still to be done, but the California condor's comeback is one of conservation's greatest **success stories**.

Golden lion tamarin numbers are on the rise,
but the species is still considered endangered.

Babies cling to their
mother's fur for the first
few weeks of their life.

Long fingers help
these primates hang
onto branches.

Golden lion tamarin

Leontopithecus rosalia

Fiery orange fur and a long, ropelike tail give the golden lion tamarin the appearance of a **fluffy toy**. We promise, however, that these monkeys are real! They live in a very **small patch of forest** on Brazil's Atlantic coast, where they leap through the treetops in family groups of two to eight. Favorite foods include fruit, bugs, lizards, and even birds.

In the 1970s golden lion tamarins were considered critically endangered, since **fewer than 200** of these marvelous monkeys remained. Since then, **captive breeding** and better protections of their **habitat** have helped improve population levels—they are 20 times what they used to be!

This species has shorter legs and thicker hooves than a domestic horse.

Przewalski's horse

Equus ferus przewalskii

The Przewalski's ("shuh-VAL-skees") horse was named after the **first person** to describe the species in modern times—**Nikołaj Przewalski**. Humans, however, have probably known about this short, stocky horse species for much longer. In fact, 20,000-year-old **cave drawings** suggest that Przewalski's horse, which today can only be found in **Mongolia**, used to roam as far away as modern-day **France**!

GALLOPING BACK

Przewalski's horses were declared extinct in the wild in the 1960s. Several decades of captive breeding have led to them being introduced back into in their native lands. Including animals in zoos and protected areas, the total population now numbers in the low thousands.

Black hair on the lower legs makes the Przewalski's horse look like it's wearing stockings!

The Przewalski's horse is as tall as an adult human and has a black, zebralike mane.

Brown bears come in many shades of brown, from light and creamy to nearly black.

MEAT AND BERRIES

Brown bears eat meat and fish when they are available, such as the salmon seen here. They also love berries, roots, plants, and insects.

In colder seasons, the brown bear eats as much as 90 lb (41 kg) of food each day,

Brown bear

Ursus arctos

Brown bears are known for being **huge, powerful predators**, but these tawny-colored titans have problems. Their range stretches **huge distances**, from North America to Asia, Europe, and even the Middle East. Many populations of brown bear have been hunted to **extinction in specific areas**, a process called **extirpation**. Sadly, many more brown bear populations, such as those in Italy, Syria, and the Himalayan region, are dangerously close to joining them.

Salmon try to swim up stream to spawn, and the bears try to catch them.

Jason Bittel

Jason is a science writer who mostly writes about animals. He tries to teach people about the life all around us, and in the process has sniffed sloth turds, trapped wild boars, swam with piranhas, and eaten stink bugs and cicadas...

Jonathan Woodward

Jonathan is an award-winning, environmentally-friendly wildlife illustrator. Much of his work is made by cutting paper from recycled magazines to create collages, although he works on his computer too. He is passionate about nature and the great outdoors.

Glossary

adapt

How a living thing changes over time to help it survive better in its environment

ancestor

Ancient relative

apocalypse

Event involving great destruction or disaster

arthropod

Group of invertebrates with a tough outer skeleton and a body divided into segments

behemoth

Huge or very powerful animal

breach

When an animal makes a complete, or almost complete, leap out of the water and splashes back down

captive breeding

Process of breeding animals in a controlled environment outside the wild

captivity

When animals are kept in a certain place by humans

climate change

Change in temperature and weather across the Earth that can be natural or caused by human activity

colonist

Person who settles in a foreign area

conservation

Protecting environments, and trying to stop plants and animals becoming extinct

DNA

Chemical that genes are made of

domestic

Animals kept as pets or on farms

Ebola virus

Infectious and deadly disease

ecosystem

Community of living things and their nonliving environment—including the soil, water, and air around them

evolve

The way living things change and adapt over time to help them survive

exploit

Use resources meanly or unfairly for your own advantage

extirpation

When a species becomes extinct in a particular area

feces

Poop

fertilize

Make soil or land better at producing crops by adding chemicals to it

gene

Part of the DNA forming coded instructions to control different cells

hatchling

Young animal that has recently emerged from i ts egg

hemisphere

Top or bottom half of the Earth

ice age

Period of time when the world is much colder, and many parts are covered in glaciers

invasive species

Animal or plant that harms an environment after humans introduce it

keratin

Tough material found in some animals. Keratin makes up hair, nails, claws, feathers, and horns

keystone species

Living thing that helps hold its habitat together

logging

Cutting down trees for their wood

marsupial

Type of mammal that is carried in its mother's pouch when it is young

matriarchal

Community of animals that is led by its female members

migrate

When animals go on a long journey to find a new place to live

native species

Species that is found in a particular place due to natural processes, such as evolution

non-native species

Species that has been introduced to an area because of human actions

Glossary

pesticide

Chemical that farmers use to control pests

photosynthesis

Process in which plants use energy from the sun to make food

pioneer

Person who is one of the first to explore a new place

poach

Kill an animal illegally to get valuable parts of it

pollinate

Transfer pollen from one plant to another so those plants can reproduce

primate

Type of mammal, which includes monkeys and humans

reproduce

Have young

rewilding

Protecting an environment by letting it go back to its natural state, such as by bringing back wild animals that used to live there

scavenger

Animal that feeds on the remains of dead animals

species

Specific types of animals or plants with shared features that can mate and produce young together

thaw

Go from frozen to liquid

traffic

Trade in something illegal

vaporize

Become gas

Index

Index

orcas 31, 84
owls 36, 54
ozone layer 16

P

pandas 13, 102–103
pangolins 14, 98, 99
passenger pigeons 36–37
penguins 33, 90–91
pesticides 101, 112
pets 63, 107
Philippine pangolins 98
photosynthesis 16, 17
pigeons 36–37
pigs 29, 57
Pinta Island tortoises 44–45
plants 15, 16, 17, 20, 21, 24,
    74, 75, 102
plastic 11, 15
poaching 71, 79, 82, 98
polar bears 72–73
pollution 11, 43
possums 64–65
prairies 15
predators 18, 34, 41, 49, 61,
    62, 73, 82, 83, 84, 91, 93, 98,
    101, 110, 118, 119
primates 54–55, 78, 79, 96–
    97, 114–115
protected areas 15
Przewalski's horses 116–117
pygmy tarsiers 12, 54–55

Q, R

quaggas 34–35
Queen Alexandra's birdwing
    80–81

rabbits 41, 110

rats 29, 50, 63
recovering animals 13, 100–
    119
recycling 15
red-crested tree-rats 68–69
rediscovered animals 12,
    46–69
red pandas 88–89
reptiles 44–45, 62–63, 76–77,
    92–93, 94–95, 106–107
rewilding 15
rhinoceroses 13, 74–75
rice farming 52
rivers 16, 52
rodents 47, 68–69
Russia 82, 104

S

saber-toothed cats 18–19
sailors 33, 45, 57
scales 53, 98, 99
scientists 8, 12, 13, 19, 22, 25,
    29, 33, 34, 35, 38, 42, 44, 47,
    48, 49, 50, 52, 53, 59, 61, 64,
    65, 66, 69, 76, 80, 85, 86, 93,
    99, 106, 110, 113
scrublands 59
seas 26, 33, 56, 93
shell 76, 107
skin 10, 43, 46, 76, 90
sloths 22–23
South Africa 34, 35, 49
South America 22, 42, 58, 65,
    69, 115
squirrels 46–47
Steller's sea cows 30–31
Sumatran rhinoceroses 75
Sunda pangolins 98

T

tails 41, 46, 48, 62, 63, 68, 85,
    88, 110, 115
takahēs 12, 60–61
Tasmanian devils 38
teeth 18, 87, 102
thylacines 38–39
toads 42–43
tortoises 44–45, 106–107
tree lobsters 50–51
trees 17, 21, 22, 36, 37, 50,
    63, 65, 88, 96, 97, 100, 115
turtles 15, 76–77
tusks 24

V, W, Z

volcanoes 8, 80
vulnerable to extinction
    (animals) 76, 93, 102

wallabies 40–41
western gorillas 79
wetlands 15
whales 14, 84–85, 108–109
whaling 108
white rhinoceroses 75
wings 28, 33, 47, 67, 80, 113
wolves 38
woolly flying squirrels 46–47
woolly mammoths 9, 24–25

zebra 34, 35, 117
zombie species 12

Acknowledgments

DK would like to thank Srijani Ganguly for proofreading, Laura Gilbert for the index, and Rachael Hare for additional icon illustrations and design work.

Also, thanks to the Lost and Found project for their inspirational stories of species conservation and rediscovery, which helped in this book:
www.lostandfoundnature.com

Picture Credits